# Flow Gently Days

Rachel Heise

En Route Books and Media, LLC
Saint Louis, MO

**⊕ENROUTE**
*Make the time*

En Route Books and Media, LLC
5705 Rhodes Avenue
St. Louis, MO 63109

Contact us at **contact@enroutebooksandmedia.com**

Cover Credit: Alford Usher Soord (1868-1915)
The Lost Sheep

Copyright 2023 Rachel Heise

ISBN-13: 979-8-88870-084-6
Library of Congress Control Number: 2023945084

All rights reserved. No part of this book may be reproduced, stored in a retrieval system, or transmitted in any form, or by any means, electronic, mechanical, photocopying, or otherwise, without the prior written permission of the author.

# Table of Contents

Prologue .................................................................... iii
Foreword by Annabelle Moseley ..................................... v
Introduction .............................................................. 1
A Crown .................................................................... 3
A Flower in the Rain ................................................... 4
Alone in Agony ........................................................... 6
Down the Aisle ........................................................... 7
Byways .................................................................... 10
Dew-Crowned Nights ................................................ 11
Discrepancy ............................................................. 13
Firelight Realm ........................................................ 14
Flow Gently Days ..................................................... 15
Haunted .................................................................. 16
I See Fire ................................................................. 17
Infinite Moments ..................................................... 19
Light-bearer ............................................................ 23
Litany of Living ........................................................ 24
Lost ........................................................................ 25
Malleable Mud ......................................................... 26
Moonlight ................................................................ 27
She Who is My Mother ............................................. 28
My Masterpiece ....................................................... 30
Perhaps .................................................................. 31
Prairie Fire .............................................................. 32

| | |
|---|---|
| Revelation | 34 |
| Roamer's Reflections | 35 |
| Sacred Beating | 37 |
| Security | 38 |
| Sentinels | 39 |
| Spatiality | 40 |
| Superabundance | 41 |
| Disarmed by Colors | 42 |
| Tear by Tear | 43 |
| The Altar of Repose in my Heart | 44 |
| The Whales | 45 |
| They Shy Away | 46 |
| Threesome Revels of Home | 47 |
| Trailblazers | 48 |
| Winter | 50 |

## Prologue

To those dear souls who peruse these words of mine, I hope some shed of light may be found from them. I write each poem as if it is the last one I will ever write, hence they fly from me to you with loving care and utter freedom. Treat them kindly please, then let them go free. For as St. Augustine once said, "The truth is like a lion; you don't have to defend it. Let it loose; it will defend itself." Peruse these at will. If there is any good in them, let it speak for itself and may your life be the better for it.

**Foreword by Annabelle Moseley**

As I began reading Rachel Heise's *Flow Gently Days,* and was greeted with the first poem, "A Crown" which teaches, "Each thorn is a little sacrifice,/A cross we must gladly bear/If we bear it well,/It blossoms into a flower," I was sitting at my desk before the statue of St. Thérèse of Lisieux. This statue was given to me by a mentor as a gift when I became a Third Order Carmelite. I could not, then, fail to whisper a prayer to The Little Flower, before I continued, for I sensed I was reading the work of a kindred soul. My instincts were confirmed in the very next poem, "A Flower in the Rain," in the second stanza with the verse, "If I was a little flower…" The poem goes on to address "my Divine Gardener," and "my Dearest Gardener," and that was when I agreed to write this foreword. After all, I had just completed writing a book that seeks to keep God prayerful company in the Garden of Gethsemane. Rachel Heise was invoking our Dearest, Divine Gardener. How could I refuse? For the call I return to again and again in my own work is the desire to stay awake with Christ, to answer the request of

Jesus in the Garden of Gethsemane, "Wilt thou not watch one hour with me?" with a resounding "Yes!" And in the work of my sister in Christ, Rachel Heise, I have found one who wants to stay awake, too.

This was confirmed when much later in the collection I encountered "The Altar of Repose in my Heart" in which the speaker is "watching, waiting… in my deepest heart," and I rejoiced. And in "Alone in Agony," I rejoiced again that this poet writes, "As I suffer my loneliness and pain, I contemplate your agony." As the speaker offers her loneliness in reparation to Jesus, these humble but powerful four lines emerge and resound with the reader:

*Small I know it is,*
*Compared to your great pain,*
*But love tells me that it will please you*
*all the same.*

That poetry summarizes the gift any ardent, awestruck, yet human, humble heart can best offer Our Lord: one which is timid in the light of God's Majesty, yet bold in the light of God's Merciful Love…

and in the light of the love we feel for the Beloved in spite of our unworthiness.

In a poem worth re-reading many times not only because it is lovely, but also because of the heft of the spiritual issue she tackles within, Heise deftly handles this state of the soul's perpetual unworthiness. This poem is the well-named "Down the Aisle," which fittingly evokes a bride, as the soul is before the Beloved. The narrative within the poem shifts from a meditation on approaching the Eucharist to one on approaching Death. In the end, the reception of the Eucharist echoes and anticipates the embrace of Our Lord at the end of our lives:

> *But for me, I practice rehearsing*
> *my last minutes on earth.*
> *For what is death,*
> *but meeting Our Lord?*
>
> *He calls me, I come running.*
> *I ask Our Lady to prepare me*
> *to be worthy of her Son.*
> *Though I'm broken,*
> *I am running into His Arms.*

*The sacred, awe-full moment draws nearer.*
*My heart is on tiptoe.*
*I am in love,*
*And long to meet my Beloved.*

*He condescends to me*
*And draws me near to Him.*
*He is All Mine, and I am all His!*

*O Jesus, Jesus, what more do I need*
*With You in my heart?*
*You Who are Everything,*
*Come to me, who am nothing.*

*For fifteen delightful minutes*
*He stays with me.*
*I am a living tabernacle*
*of the Most High God!*

A standout in this collection includes the stellar "Infinite Moments" which reads as though the poet held up a butterfly net in the middle of the Traditional Mass, catching the inherent poetry of the Mass of the Ages like so many winged moments of transcendent beauty. Latin words are interspersed throughout the poem with resonance, and the verses sing. At her best, Heise's poetry is authentic prayer in which "Holy angels throng the air,/ with unseen adoration, unheard jubilation" and the poet, invoking the assistance of the Blessed Virgin asks, "may my poor tongue paint a dim shadow of this glory: The Holy Sacrifice of the Mass."

The poet's tongue is the thing, is it not? The poet is a teller, a tailor, of words. And yet Heise arrives at a greater truth in this stanza: the truth that each of us who receives Our Lord has upon each one of our "poor tongue[s]" a "dim shadow of this glory," the glory that Jesus Himself has come to dwell thereon. Poets of old would be called "golden-tongued" when they spun language and metaphor with great skill. St. John Chrysostom was named "golden mouthed" because of his eloquence...but he is also known as the "Doctor of the Eucharist." May each tongue that receives Our Lord be honeyed with beauty and goodness in speech... and imbued with love. It is deeply meaningful that Heise has tied both impressions together in one poem with a prayer that asks for the "poor tongue" to "paint a dim shadow of this glory." Amen!

St. Thérèse of Lisieux wrote, "Let us go forward in peace, our eyes upon heaven, the only one goal of our labors." This collection allows the reader greater peace as it is fixed firmly upon the goal of heaven. Do more than simply read and savor the many moments of beauty found in this collection. Pray along with Rachel Heise.

—Annabelle Moseley, author of *Awake with Christ: Living the Catholic Holy Hour in Your Home (How Keeping God Prayerful Company in the Garden of Gethsemane can Change Your Life)*

## Introduction

The thought of my setting out to write a book of poems would be in itself far too daunting a task to my mind. Yet the thing that motivates me to continue giving voice to my perception of the scenes that go on around me and within each of our lives is the truth that pervades all of creation: that life is worth living. In this way, each poem I write is as unexpected as the next. I merely try to be alert to the divine glorious moments in time that often pass by underappreciated. It is to be on the lookout for a trail of lights that lead back to our Heavenly Father and remind me there is still so much good to be found. "Every best gift, and every perfect gift, is from above, coming down from the Father of lights, with whom there is no change, nor shadow of alteration." - James 1:17

The places that I have found most conducive to writing poetry have been anything from a local train ride home, to scribbling out my heart's song on a scrap piece of paper while cooking in a collegiate kitchen, to late night reveries into the wee hours of the morning. Most of my composition process of wrangling words into their due and proper place perhaps happens before I am even cognizant of it. For when I set out to write, the poem flows like my heart is already intimately familiar with every word. As I let the words sift through my head, they dance into their place as delighted as I am to behold them.

Although my poems reflect on a wide variety of life experiences, they are not strictly factual. I tend to be constantly mulling over recurring themes that are happening in my life or those I see; thus, the transmission of the poem gets imbued with a little bit of love and lightheartedness along the way. To live is to love deeply and to not be afraid to lose. Time waits for us to see it in this way: an invitation to set out and to return. I hope my poems may reflect a small piece of this truly sacred invitation to participate in temporality for what endures.

## A Crown

*All of us have a crown to wear.*
*When we first begin to wear it,*
*It is a crown of thorns,*
*before it is transformed.*

*Each thorn is a little sacrifice,*
*A cross we must gladly bear.*
*If we bear it well,*
*It blossoms into a flower!*

*If day by day we suffer well,*
*Then in the end it will become*
*Not a crown of shame,*
*But a lovely crown of glory.*

*Thus by some sweet alchemy,*
*We turn life's troubles into blessings,*
*Curses into graces,*
*And thorns into sweet flowers.*

## A Flower in the Rain

*Between the showers of rain,*
*the sunshine peeps through the clouds,*
*bathing the land in its sweet warmth.*
*Encouraging the plants and flowers to grow,*
*and stretch forth evermore,*
*tall, and strong, and true.*

*If I was a little flower,*
*you would be the sun*
*that helped me on my way*
*when life was dark indeed.*

*You helped me to grow out of my bud,*
*so that I might blossom*
*and grow gently into a full flower.*
*Each in your own way,*
*you helped me in this way.*
*Even though perhaps sometimes*
*you were more like the rain.*

*Just as the dark and dreary rainy days*
*are necessary to make plants grow,*
*my Divine Gardener knew just how*
*to season my life with bitter rain*
*and sweet joy with pain.*

*Thank you for being there for me,*
*in those dark and dreary times,*
*perhaps you'll never know how much*
*you helped me in those times.*

*And now my Dearest Gardener,*
*wishes to pluck His little flower,*
*and have her for Himself.*
*There with Him I'll pray for you,*
*as I hope you will for me.*
*Thank you for helping me,*
*to blossom like a flower in the rain.*

## **Alone in Agony**

*As I suffer my loneliness and pain,
I contemplate Your agony,
You suffered me that night
all alone.*

*You were steeped in pain,
through and through,
yet no one was there
to comfort You.*

*I wish somehow to comfort You,
By cheerfully submitting to this pain.
With humble gratitude,
I offer You my loneliness,
As a consolation for that night of agony
You spent for me all alone.*

*Small I know it is,
Compared to your great pain,
But love tells me that it will please you
all the same.
Just as in that garden,
When you accepted the Will of the Father,
I add my own "Amen".
"Not my Will, but Thine be Done!"*

## **Down the Aisle**

*I walk down the aisle.*
*Feeling my nothingness,*
*I grasp for Our Lady's Hand.*
*She is there;*
*she is always there.*

*I picture myself hand in Hand with Mary.*
*She is guiding me and helping me.*
*Down the aisle I see Jesus,*
*in the disguise of the Eucharist,*
*feeding us poor lambs.*

*He comes full of love and goodness.*
*Who will open their heart to Him,*
*As well as their mouth?*

*But for me, I practice rehearsing*
*my last minutes on earth.*
*For what is death,*
*but meeting Our Lord?*

*He calls me, I come running.*
*I ask Our Lady to prepare me*
*to be worthy of her Son.*
*Though I'm broken,*
*I am running into His Arms.*

*The sacred, awe-full moment draws nearer.*
*My heart is on tiptoe.*
*I am in love,*
*And long to meet my Beloved.*

*He condescends to me*
*And draws me near to Him.*
*He is All Mine, and I am all His!*

*O Jesus, Jesus, what more do I need*
*With You in my heart?*
*You Who are Everything,*
*Come to me, who am nothing.*

*For fifteen delightful minutes*
*He stays with me.*
*I am a living tabernacle*
*of the Most High God!*

*Then one last tender embrace*
*And He leaves me.*
*I go forth once more*
*to fight the good fight.*
*Though we must part,*
*we are always united in heart.*

*And I wait and hope for*
*The Day, the Eternal Embrace,*

*When I shall see Him face-to Face!*
*And I work and pray and do my best,*
*And I love Him with all*
*the might of my little heart.*

*Jesus, I love You, help me to see like You see, and to love like You love. Amen.*

## Byways

*When I met you grace*
*fell like molten embers,*
*then I knew you and you pierced*
*my puzzled masterpiece,*
*till I took a chance on you.*

*I saw the resiliency of your heart,*
*a heart I could only hope*
*to hold and cherish always.*
*Yet, alas, through all the byways!*

*At first you scared me, yet intrigued me*
*a deadly duo:*
*I feared for you*
*even as I cared for you.*

*Then I felt ill equipped to love you,*
*Baffling, ever felt like trifling.*
*And I steered clear of love.*
*Harm oft wears vestiges of caution.*
*Impatience becomes inaction.*

*Now I stand more aware*
*and startlingly clear,*
*Yet that Light which shines on me dazzling:*
*shines still, unwavering, ever pervading.*

## **Dew-Crowned Nights**

*These grace-filled breaths I gasp*
*claim existence against the plight*
*through the callous air that is*
*fraught with blight and fright.*

*Poised with a death-grip stance*
*as a warrior in a brazen night*
*hazy-filled with renegade flames*
*and jilted dew from the fight.*

*Dancing and side-stepping*
*With every breath so few*
*For too long, far too long,*
*Have I then fought you.*

*No more, Fire, will I condescend*
*to dance this dance with you.*
*This season I will claim for my own*
*and return to sunshiny-lit days*
*followed by dew crowned nights.*
*The brilliant glory of things nonsense*
*the sturdy serenity I know awaits me,*
*admit me once again into your happy fold.*
*Yet in coming undone, let me not undo them.*

*I now beg you, as I lay down my arms*
*And join your band of happy few*
*let not me come unawares*
*to singe them with my very tears.*

## Discrepancy

*An artist's blessing, an artist's curse.*
*You see sunrays, I see prisms full of rainbows.*
*You see shadows, I see reflections and illusions of images traced.*
*You hear bugs, I hear a summer symphony.*

*How can I blame you for not being able to handle me,*
*when often I don't know how to handle me myself?*
*How can I blame you for calling me a contradiction,*
*when I wish as much as you that a contradiction I would not be?*

*A convoluted stream of eager passions, feeble prayers,*
*and a history as contradictory races through my head,*
*as full of confusing painful memories as unbelievable blessings.*
*I cudgel my mind and heart, but I will never fit in.*

*I am not tame, I can only hope to be more good.*
*But wild I'll always be.*
*I am not like the rest of you and I can't expect you to understand me.*
*Please at least keep trying.*
*A curse and a blessing,*
*A struggle and a strength.*
*Forgive me and help me to understand me.*
*No, I do not ask you to understand me,*
*just be there with me and don't let me scare you away.*
*I need you more than you know.*

## **Firelight Realm**

*As glowing embers leaping into the celestial realm,*
*the molten leaves like ships of gold sailing high into the breeze.*
*Born high above into the windswept sky,*
*fragrant with crackling pine and dew.*
*All imbued with a smoky incense*
*of full hearts and young ambitions.*

*The melody of youthful voices,*
*mingles with the crackling of the burning timber.*
*These youthful truth-seekers rest*
*and the world beyond the firelight ceases to exist,*
*save as a beautiful backdrop from another realm.*

*They sing and laugh and chatter*
*and the murmur of their voices together,*
*leaves an indelible echo*
*for future ages to catch*
*and add their own refrain.*

*The sparks fly up like gentle fireflies,*
*Dancing in ecstasy and pure joy,*
*Stars above and hills around*
*Look down as if to say,*
*"Laugh now for it is your hour,*
*Time can wait and dreams shall fly."*

## Flow Gently Days

*I let your life change mine when your hand slipped into*
*my life.*
*The power of one human grasp broke through my barriers.*
*Letting go but still holding back; my tide fails to turn.*
*I fear I've been cruelly cautious.*
*Precious labor: what awe-filled responsibility*
*Trembling at the thought that I hold your heart in mine.*
*Heart, fall gently, and bear thee well.*

*I dreamed of running someday soon*
*then found I was flying.*
*Each day I add a new hue to my dreams;*
*the contour deepening with the passing of the days.*

*Let the rolling of the years flow gently upon me;*
*charged with beauty and pain,*
*beauty and grace.*
*Flow gently days, and do not pass me by unchanged.*
*Hands of mine have a care, and break not this heart of mine.*
*If I break mine, yours goes with it.*

## Haunted

*Haunted by the past, or is it the present,*
*which pins down those airy feathers,*
*meant for power and grace*
*and very pride of place?*

*Is the chain one singular, yet to be divided,*
*Stumbled over, neglected, ever-present?*
*I am not the one you need perhaps.*
*My love does not have that power:*
*to mend the loose and fray the knotted.*

*You say true love breaks chains*
*But whose is the truest?*
*I fear for you as much as I love you.*
*When great hearts pant in stifled lives,*
*some person must pay the due. Who?*

## I See Fire

*She always had that something about her eyes.*
*You could never just look into her eyes and pass unchanged.*
*Those eyes so demure, yet so terrifying*
*as if holding unfathomable secrets*
*or some soul-searching truth better left unknown.*
*Those eyes held a fire*
*lit from some unknown source.*

*What could start such a fire*
*and what could fuel it so?*
*It bursts, it burns,*
*but never devours.*
*It fades and dims,*
*but never goes out.*
*A steady glow pervades her being*
*ever anon and anew.*
*Looking into such mysterious eyes, begs the question:*
*what have they seen that makes them so?*

*What have I seen you ask? Do you really wish to know?*
*Or if I tell you will you walk away like all the rest?*

*I have seen truth taught by a bittersweet teacher*
*but scarred into my consciousness, stark and unrelenting.*

*I have seen a beauty so infinite it hurts.*

*I have seen a dream I thought I knew shattered
and then rebuilt oh so gently to be so much more.*

*This fire that courses through my veins
I can't explain to you.
If I showed you, you might get burned
and I could not live with that.
But still sparks are bound to escape myself.
Sparks of uncomfortable challenge
or challenging comfort;
to each his own.
Please don't back down. Please don't leave me.*

## **Infinite Moments**

*"Introibo ad altare Dei..."*
*(I will go in unto the Altar of God...)*

*Sweet Mother, how can I describe this*
*great wonder and mystery of redemption?*
*It will always be an indescribable mystery,*
*but may my poor tongue paint a dim shadow*
*of this glory: The Holy Sacrifice of the Mass.*

*The priest, the servers, and the people*
*become one.*
*Each with a place; each with a mission.*
*One in the Mystical Body of Christ.*
*One in the Voice of the Church.*

*The Mass bridges centuries,*
*yet remains ever ancient, ever new.*
*It crosses nations,*
*yet remains always near and dear.*

*When we are there,*
*it is like nothing else really matters.*

*Petty problems pale,*
*and become absorbed into the Divine Cosmos.*
*Catching inklings of life seen from*
*a divine perspective,*
*we find life is bearable after all.*
*And we begin again.*

*Grace is poured forth relentlessly,*
*we feel the power.*
*Every fiber of our being is at attention.*
*We are ready to give anything,*
*but rest content in the moment.*
*We are on fire,*
*but we are at peace.*

*Holy angels throng the air,*
*with unseen adoration, unheard jubilation.*
*And you, dear Mother, are there too,*
*assisting the priest with the Holy Sacrifice.*
*Form him, dear Mother, into a priest*
*according to the Heart of your own Son.*
*Form us too, spotless Virgin,*
*make our offering of our imperfect selves*
*pure and pleasing in His sight.*

*Pleading longingly we cry,*
*"Kyrie, Kyrie Eleison!"*
*full of hope, full of trust.*
*We need you, Jesus, so.*
*Then ringing out confidently*
*in one full voice we exclaim,*
*"Gloria in Excelsis Deo,*
*et in terra pax hominibus bonae voluntatis!"*

*This is our Faith,*
*the faith we proudly proclaim,*
*the faith of our fathers,*
*the faith of the Saints,*
*and of our hearts:*
*"Credo in Unum Deum…"*

*One with the angels we sing*
*those heavenly ancient words,*
*"Sanctus, Sanctus, Sanctus…"*

*With softened hearts, we pray for peace*
*sorely needed for a broken world,*
*"Agnus Dei, qui tollis peccata mundi,*
*dona nobis pacem."*

*Time has stepped into Eternity.*
*Heaven has come down to Earth.*
*We have felt the pulse of Christ's Own Heart,*
*which has pressed suffering humanity*
*close to it's Savior's breast.*

*We have assisted at The Sacrifice of All Time,*
*which is seamless, yet full of infinite moments.*

## **Light-bearer**

*A broken world lies around us,*
*aching and full of endless searches,*
*never finding hope, never finding peace.*

*Who knows the sleepless nights,*
*who knows the broken hearts so well,*
*so well, except for You?*

*Jesus, we need you. I need you,*
*Accept my love for you on their behalf.*
*They know not what they do.*
*Have mercy, Jesus, have mercy on us.*

*May I be a steady light for them*
*in their darkness, burning with gentle zeal.*
*That they may have at least*
*one beacon of truth and goodness.*
*A holocaust of love, poured out for the world.*
*May I show them your love*
*and bring them your peace.*
*Amen.*

## Litany of Living

*Playing peekaboo with memories,*
*returning again and again,*
*reliving them and regaining them.*
*All is not lost but found in Him.*

*Losing the chain of thought,*
*finding the whispers,*
*and exposing them to the Father,*
*not caring to affront but to uplift.*

*Fancying to play with mosaics,*
*pebbles in the sand.*
*What translucent nothings,*
*tell a story all their own.*

*The tide turns but it shall return,*
*for thus it always has,*
*and thus it always will.*

*Patterns in the mystery*
*lead us home,*
*to a place of encounter,*
*a trysting of risk and peace.*

## **Lost**

*I am lost on a dark sea,*
*floundering in infinitude,*
*One star alone shines above,*
*Like a portal back to realitude.*

*I hear voices calling, faint and far.*
*The fog is thick around my face,*
*yet their refrains seem like*
*clarion calls piercing through my daze.*

*My heart is deafened by the silent chaos.*
*Wilt thou extend a hand to me,*
*so that in the sunlit lands*
*I will return with thee to be?*

*Graciously let the presence of one warm grasp,*
*free me from this infinitude of finitude,*
*lay siege to this prison of floundering fears,*
*so that in peace I may surely fly into beatitude.*

## **Malleable Mud**

*Let me speak of my friend the mud,*
*though malleable, impressionable,*
*It remembers its purpose, its value.*

*Though attentive to the pitter-patter*
*of newfound freedom,*
*exaltation of returning sun,*
*in each scurry, in each trill of high glee.*

*Tread so underfoot mud feels the tremors*
*of faint hearts fearing to breath deep,*
*Amid the rustic undertone of bravehearts.*

*Mud feels these things and yet it passes through.*
*As if knowing the art of loving and leaving hurt behind,*
*It turns the echoes of shivers into a living poem.*
*A poema: I was here, I listened, and forged true.*

## **Moonlight**

*Twilight fades, transient hour,*
*to bid adieu for a higher grace*
*of gentleness to come to place:*
*Verily, the passage of the moon.*

*Beneath the airy gleams pervading,*
*lies a world forgetting how to sleep;*
*O weary pilgrim, forget your peep,*
*Come listen to the enfolding tune.*

*Since time original was heard to be,*
*that long the Gentle Watcher of the Night*
*has ruled over both serene and afright.*
*Let grayness cease; clarity be as noon.*

*In peace and not in trembling,*
*Let our thoughts be duly found,*
*For if sought for by our Hound,*
*will we beg, "Lord, it is too soon"?*

*Too soon? Then let us cherish,*
*And learn how to abide and reside,*
*To appreciate He who doth provide,*
*and begin under beams of His own moon.*

## She Who is My Mother

*I sing of the Lady,*
*that I call Mother.*
*She is lovely and good,*
*simple and sweet.*

*Like me she is a human,*
*but by God's grace*
*she is His Mother.*
*We call her Queen of Heaven,*
*but also as of Earth.*

*God gave her to me*
*to help me get to Heaven.*
*One day I too will die.*
*On that day I hope*
*that she will come to me.*

*Then will she lead me*
*by the hand, straight to*
*her Son's open arms.*
*The moment of all moments,*
*the long-desired embrace.*

*There for all eternity,*
*will I sing my thanks*
*and praise to God.*
*Then I will plead for*
*all mortal man's need.*
*Safe forever in His Arms*
*with His Mother and Mine.*

## My Masterpiece

*You ask Me, "When will it be done?*
*How much longer must we wait?*
*All of us are eager to see the*
*finished piece."*

*Wait, wait, and be patient,*
*my dear little ones.*
*The time will come when it will come.*
*Do not pry back the canvas*
*and try to peek behind to see*
*before the finished and appointed time.*

*You hear strange sounds;*
*you think something must be wrong.*
*Do you doubt my skill*
*as the Artist of You All?*
*All of it is necessary,*
*wait and you will see…*

## Perhaps

*Perhaps, perhaps I had my focus all wrong,*
*Perhaps I thought more of me and not of you.*
*Perhaps I didn't realize how much*
*you needed me to just be there for you.*
*The fact is that you deserve it,*
*regardless of what you've done for me.*

*And for what you've done for me,*
*I will be always grateful.*
*I pray you remember me*
*in the dark times, in the hard times.*
*When you need a voice to call you back,*
*a hand to hold, and a heart*
*waiting to be there for you.*

## Prairie Fire

*A fire sweeps across the prairie,*
*Devouring the long billowing grasses,*
*Burning the sweet wild-flowers.*
*Leaving behind a seemingly dead land.*

*But hope lies hidden in the dry soil,*
*Yes, hope, is waiting for the new season.*
*Though to the outward eye all seems lost,*
*Hope is waiting in the soil.*

*Sometimes our lives seem as if*
*Our souls have undergone a prairie fire.*
*As if nothing is left and*
*we are tempted to give up.*
*We think, "How can I carry on; all seems lost?"*

*But hope lies just on the horizon,*
*Bidding it's time patiently,*
*Longing for the hour of revival.*
*Waiting in the darkness of the dry soil.*
*Just like the prairie soil,*
*If we hope on and are faithful,*
*Life will spring up again*
*after the Refiner's fire.*

*The grass will grow tall and slender once more,*
*the sweet wildflowers will spring up once more,*
*sending out their fragrance on the wild wind.*

*The prairie is not lost forever*
*in a lifeless stupor; life has returned.*
*It has been purified, rejuvenated, and revived.*
*Hope, that wonderful seed, lay hidden in the soil,*
*Waiting to be unleashed.*

## Revelation

*It defies analyzation,*
*calling for love or dismissal.*
*It is in the very moment,*
*when you cease to love it:*
*that it ceases to reveal itself.*
*To those who have ears,*
*let them hear the sweet melody.*

## **Roamer's Reflections**

*I look up at the stars twinkling above me
Beaming at me as gently as ever they did before.
Only now their celestial radiance is dimmed,
by the tears glistening in my eyes.*

*I look down from my mountain perch
upon my home of yesteryears,
For home it will always be,
Knowing that I cannot return
For I am not the one I used to be.*

*The night wind brings dear memories of that gentle sacred place,
Where I was nurtured and loved
In the hillside glens and woods of my yesteryears.*

*Till that one day when my very foundations were tested
and found whether they were worth standing upon.
Until the heart of a warrior emerged in full force
but too much for the little people to comprehend.*

*I used to think things were always black and white,
And never grey or blue.
But then I found unexpected greatness in the unlikeliest
places.*

*The same struggle of goodness and strife going on in*
*every human heart*
*Wars and peace that they never could have imagined.*

*O dreary world break thy wreckage instead on me,*
*and let my homeland unsullied be.*
*Let their simple lives, loves and*
*blissful fantasies remain*
*and unscathed be.*
*I journey on and will bleed for thee.*

*I smile and my sigh of homesickness is chased away by*
*the knowledge*
*of victories hard won*
*and the warmth of stranger people*
*met and loved.*
*Destined to roam but happier this way*
*The earth is mine and everything in it.*

## **Sacred Beating**

*Bursting the wrinkled skin,*
*Then now raw and pulsing,*
*Gapping, gory and gasping.*

*What frail vessels we are*
*To carry the mighty flood*
*Of divine love within us.*

*We would yet break if, oh,*
*we could not, would not,*
*grow beyond our old confines.*

*What beautiful wreckage,*
*invincible loveliness,*
*sacred beating bold.*

## **Security**

*Far more lasting sensation,*
*than turrets of silver,*
*or the timpani of royals,*
*found with you is security.*

*To be loved by you,*
*is to be embraced by serenity.*
*To be held by constancy,*
*Swooned by subsistence.*

## **Sentinels**

*There is a realm of sorrow,*
*that draws a veil against*
*the recesses of man's heart.*
*Guardians of grief, stand by:*
*and be watchers of the night.*

*Holy hours of the blessed night,*
*bestow your gracious timelessness,*
*and ease man's shaking voice.*

*Sentinels like shining towers*
*upon the hills…*
*Remind us of what endures,*
*and hold out the light to us.*

## Spatiality

*I wonder at our fragility,*
*the plight of our humanity;*
*to be such bearers of love,*
*encompassed by unpredictability.*

*Truly to desire is to live,*
*to aspire is vulnerability,*
*a choice of receptivity,*
*poised between two goods.*

*And yet our weakness confounds us,*
*sets us apart in our resiliency,*
*opening us to grace,*
*and sense of due place.*

*Perhaps time is a beacon,*
*training us for spatiality.*
*Honed to this liberality,*
*Mystery unlocks presence.*

## **Superabundance**

*Not to be content with satiety,*
*but to crave superabundance.*
*In avoiding presence lies futility,*
*a void of all that claims breath.*

*Every moment in itself a mystery,*
*test of our vulnerability inviting,*
*a source of unending fecundity.*
*To soar into surrender open.*

*Being has two destinations,*
*the crucial juncture of love:*
*tragedy and viviality,*
*bridged only by this word: hope.*

*Hope, renewing our identity,*
*replacing our obsessions,*
*returning true vulnerability*
*to its presence as grace.*

*Summation of our frivolity,*
*is never beyond placement,*
*we know our vagrant triviality,*
*is but encompassed by Him alone.*

## Disarmed by Colors

*Dimming the tapers she beckons,*
*vesting our senses in surrender,*
*By defenseless wonder armed,*
*Step lightly and do not doubt.*

*Accompanied by artless wonder,*
*Initiated into the nightly revels,*
*Hues and shades they also,*
*participate in creation's hymn.*

*Even absence of color holds space,*
*For an epiphany of recognition,*
*For a home of indomitable grace.*
*Honoring transcendent realities.*

## Tear by Tear

*Pouring all the struggles,*
*frustrations, and pains,*
*of the past months,*
*into the bosom of Jesus, who*
*never misses a tear.*

*Each tear, cleansing, falls*
*and drops treasured into*
*the hands of Him who knew*
*heartache best.*

*Each tear, a cherished symbol,*
*of the efforts of a little heart,*
*to do great things.*

*Then resting gently, spent,*
*in the arms of Jesus,*
*who counts every tear,*
*and calms every fear.*

## The Altar of Repose in my Heart

*I am keeping watch.*
*Watching, waiting…*
*With Him, for Him.*

*All around me is turmoil,*
*but in my deepest heart*
*the candles are lit:*
*defying the darkness*
*and waiting for the dawn.*

*In my deepest heart,*
*I give my best and biggest flowers.*
*All for Him.*

*Yes, in this small corner,*
*it is sad and desolate,*
*but hopeful.*

*I will be faithful*
*in the confusion,*
*and by my trust*
*console Jesus.*
*As long as He pleases,*
*in whatever way He chooses,*
*till the Resurrection's blessed hour.*

## **The Whales**

*Cerebral blue lifts you up,*
*and draws you in near.*
*As crystalline equilibrium,*
*most radiant and dear.*

*Labyrinthian miles go by,*
*Fog billows sweep across,*
*Deep entrenchments till,*
*the sagacious water's edge.*

*Noble creatures of the deep,*
*live two worlds in between:*
*Subterranean sagaciousness,*
*beneath the evanescent expanse.*

*Fearful strokes scratch the surface,*
*scuttling about in courier boats.*
*Calling for a transcendent pause,*
*to plunge beneath impervious.*

## They Shy Away

*They shy away as if you taint their world,*
*and a bittersweet melody trails behind you.*
*Infringing upon them,*
*as if a taunt to their simple life.*

*Wounded, I know not how to heal myself.*
*Weeping, I pass haunted by pain.*
*Alone, is there no one to pause and weep a while with me?*

*Weep with me and take me by the hand.*
*Perhaps we could have just as well*
*changed place.*
*And I would reach out to break the wall of pain.*

## **Threesome Revels of Home**

*Set out and query this, what is*
*familiar enough to feel real,*
*special enough to be significant?*
*Invested in a sphere of wholeness.*

*Who is she that is found here?*
*The Hearthfire must be kept,*
*for enduring trust to abide.*
*Vigilance fosters security.*

*Who is she mighty at rest?*
*The Helpmeet holding life,*
*with devotion plenty rife.*
*Nurturing all to flourish.*

*Who is she beloved twiced?*
*The Hope flows on beyond,*
*to eddies sundry unknown,*
*Some muddy, some sweet.*

*Unstinting, it is she!*
*For her, three words mind;*
*these she revels in for*
*no man shall take these from her.*

## Trailblazers

*To go out to the wide open glorious unknown,*
*so unsure and yet so hopeful.*

*Do I dare, do I try?*
*What would happen if I stayed?*
*Should I? Could I if I tried?*
*Something in me was made for more*
*I know*
*My wings grow and yet are cramped.*
*My breath grows stronger and yet is stifled here.*
*Am I so wrong? Will I ever find a place that I fit in?*

*Stay here in this dear place or go where fate will send me?*
*A higher power will guide the way I know and yet why do I stand here on this shore,*
*Afraid to set sail but looking back I know my time here is no more.*

*The sea breeze blows around me.*
*Calling me, sweetly haunting me,*
*night and day, all the way.*
*Was I not born to sail the seven seas?*
*This harbor reeks of yesteryears.*

*Succumb to a life half-lived or pursue a life fully alive?*
*The waves beat against the shore; beat against my heart.*
*Like a steady knocking on the door or the beating of the*
*drums for war.*
*To stay or to go?*

*I want to live with reckless abandon.*
*To love with abandon, to worship with authenticity,*
*to dream relentlessly, to work with purpose,*
*to create boldly, to enjoy life with zest.*
*To be or not to be?*

*I will hold my old friends ever in my heart; all so dear, so true.*
*Remember my heritage, bend some rules perhaps.*
*Explore new horizons, challenge the status quo.*
*Create as much beauty in this*
*world as one girl honestly can.*

*I will grow; I will change. Tis all so true*
*But still ever remain quintessentially*
*Me.*

*To be or not to be?*

*To be a trailblazer I will be.*

## **Winter**

*In bridal raiment bedecked,*
*glittering in the suspense,*
*in air so clear it sings,*
*of trust so sweet it rings.*

*While above the chorus soars,*
*dancing in the spirit of promise,*
*burrowed under blankets of truth,*
*lies a stronghold ready to give.*

*The footpath through the snow,*
*seals the fate of the solitary foe.*
*Against heavy snow is welded*
*a sign of intent more purposeful.*

*Swirling, gnawing wintry blast,*
*knows not the secret held within,*
*in the practice of love made strong,*
*from abundance to creative fidelity.*

*The time of color has passed,*
*when all is awash in sunset,*
*the preparations have been laid,*
*well-stocked and provisioned.*

*Now is the time of vision,*
*undimmed by disarray,*
*to trust that your good deeds,*
*will be brought to their completion.*

oduct-compliance

www.ingramcontent.com/pod-product-compliance
Lightning Source LLC
Chambersburg PA
CBHW060429050426
42449CB00009B/2211